Join Hands!
The Ways We Celebrate Life

Pat Mora *with photographs by* **George Ancona**

⌂ Charlesbridge

"Join hands!" is what we say.

We sing canciones, too.

We plan a hoopla day.

We strut and ballyhoo.

We plan a masquerade.

Some read, some ballyhoo.

Friends join a pet parade.

So plan your masquerade.

Surprise your friends with fun.

Create your own parade.

Join hands with everyone.

Surprise your friends with fun.

Start now and take a chance.

Join hands with everyone,

and your feet begin their dance.

Start now and take a chance.

Find your special, private beat.

Let your feet begin their dance

when you're *skipping* down the *street*.

Find your special, private beat.

"Amigos, join hands!" we'll say

when we're prancing down the street

in our happy, hoopla way.

A pantoum (pan-TOOM) is a repeating form written in four-line stanzas (quatrains). The second and fourth lines in one stanza become the first and third lines in the next stanza. In the last stanza, the second and fourth lines are almost the same as the first and third lines of the first stanza. So, like a group of friends joining hands, the poem becomes a circle. I liked playing with the form and hope you'll enjoy writing your own repeating poems.

Join Hands!

"Join hands!" is what we say.
We sing canciones, too.
We plan a hoopla day.
We strut and ballyhoo.

Sometimes we sing soft, too.
We plan a masquerade.
Some read, some ballyhoo.
Friends join a pet parade.

So plan your masquerade.
Surprise your friends with fun.
Create your own parade.
Join hands with everyone.

Surprise your friends with fun.
Start now and take a chance.
Join hands with everyone,
and your feet begin their dance.

Start now and take a chance.
Find your special, private beat.
Let your feet begin their dance
when you're skipping down the street.

Find your special, private beat.
"Amigos, join hands!" we'll say
when we're prancing down the street
in our happy, hoopla way.

Author's Note

The talented photographer George Ancona and I have enjoyed creating this book that celebrates the pleasure of quiet moments and of rejoicing with friends and family. I chose the pantoum, which is based on a Malaysian poetic form, because I so like its repetition and energy. It reminds me of the rhythm and energy of young people when they sing or dance or play.

George and I have been fortunate to travel within and outside of this country, and we feel blessed to have heard many languages and to have experienced many cultures. We are bilingual and wish we were trilingual. We believe in the human family and hope you do, too. Join hands with us in celebrating your individual uniqueness and celebrating our wonderful diversity.

Photographer's Note

My thanks go to all the friends, teachers, principals, directors, parents, and all the children who helped make this book a reality: Russell Baker and Emily Lowman of The National Dance Institute of New Mexico; John Chamberlain, Oceana Holton, Tara Chandler, and Brenden Schafer of The Fayette Street Academy; Elaine Hausman, Pearl Potts, and Amanda Lujan of The Children's Dance Program; Chris Wells of the All Species Projects; Pete's Pets; Laura Castille of The Cesar Chavez Elementary School; Elijah and Maria Whippo and The Clan Tynker; Laura McCloskey and Isidro Urtiaga of the Little Earth School; Kelly Huber, director of the Santa Fe Youth Symphony and the Mozart Mariachi Program, and Jose Santiago and Raul Ojeda, directors of the Mariachi Program; Benny Lujan and the Buffalo Dancers of the Ice Mountain Dance Group; Adrienne Bellis and Belisama Irish Dance; Jon Robinson and the ice skaters of the Genoveva Chavez Community Center; Jamira and Nicholas Cordova and their parents; and Isella Gonzales and her twins. And to Vern Scarborough for taking our picture.

George

For my agent, Elizabeth Harding, and her assistant, Anna Webman—P. M.

To Jay, L. A., and Amanda Maisel—G. A.

Text copyright © 2008 by Pat Mora
Illustrations copyright © 2008 by George Ancona
All rights reserved, including the right of reproduction in whole or in part in any form.
Charlesbridge and colophon are registered trademarks of Charlesbridge Publishing, Inc.

Published by Charlesbridge
85 Main Street
Watertown, MA 02472
(617) 926-0329
www.charlesbridge.com

Library of Congress Cataloging-in-Publication Data
Mora, Pat.
    Join hands! / Pat Mora; photographs by George Ancona.
        p. cm.
    ISBN 978-1-58089-202-5 (reinforced for library use)
    ISBN 978-1-58089-203-2 (softcover)
I. Ancona, George, ill. II. Title.
PS3563.073J65 2007
811'.54—dc22   2007027024

Printed in China
(hc) 10 9 8 7 6 5 4 3 2 1
(sc) 10 9 8 7 6 5 4 3 2 1

Display type set in P22 Aglio, designed by Kevin Kegler, developed from
        letterforms originally painted by muralist/artist Tanya Zabinski.
Text type set in Billy, designed by David Buck for SparkyType, New Zealand
Color separations by Chroma Graphics, Singapore
Printed and bound by Regent Publishing Services
Production supervision by Brian G. Walker
Designed by Susan Mallory Sherman